CULTURE SHOCK

DR. KATRINA SWEET

Foreword by Dr. Danny F. Ellis

CULTURE SHOCK

For information, please visit our Web site at
www.pendiumpublishing.com

PENDIUM Publishing and its logo
are registered trademarks.

Culture Shock
by Katrina Sweet

Copyright © Katrina Sweet, 2014
All Rights Reserved.

ISBN: 978-1-936513-98-7

PUBLISHER'S NOTE

Dedication

I dedicate this book to my precious children, Tashika and Kevin. Everything I do, I do for you. You have taught me what unconditional love really is. Thank you for your patience while I learned what being a mother was all about. I pray one day that I am blessed to be a better grandmother and fill in all the gaps I did not fill as a mother. I pray God's blessings over the both of you. I believe every word God has promised concerning you. I rest in Numbers 23:19; (God is not a man, that He should lie, nor a son of man that He should change His mind. Does He speak and then not act? Does He promise and not fulfill?) Continue to look to the hills from whence cometh your help. All of your help comes from the Lord. Always remember that mommy loves you today and forever!

You may ask the question, "Why did she decide to write this book." I asked myself the same question a thousand times. After weeks of struggling with the idea of what others might think or say if I published this book, I decided to move forward. One, the constant reminder of the competitiveness that occur between women which leads to rivalry and malicious attacks known as indirect aggression would not let me forfeit the opportunity to bring awareness to this topic. Second, the viciousness that emerges among black women within the workplace, homes, churches, and communities, is literally destroying the black race. In no way am I attempting to denigrate black women. I am a woman, and yes, I am black. Besides, black women have suffered enough by fault or default, and do not need to be subjected to criticism or slander. However, I must admit, some of us need a reality check.

Please do not misconstrue my intent. I do not dislike women nor do I dislike being a woman. I find pleasure in being a woman. I enjoy who God created me to be. Nevertheless, I must be transparent with you. Sometimes the only solace I have in being a woman is found in Psalm 139: 13-14 (For you created my inmost being; you knit me together in my mother's womb. I praise you because I am fearfully and wonderfully made; your works are wonderful, I know that full well). The constant negativity about black women and my personal experiences have caused deep inroads to my bank of positivity, and I am often left feeling empty and drained. There is not a day that goes by that I am not reminded of the cruelty and brutishness of black women. As a woman, my nature is to defend or offer some type of explanation; however, it is very difficult to do so as women without failure find a way to add credence to the idioms.

Recently, I was introduced to the behavior called "indirect aggression". Although I did not fully understand what was happening, one thing for sure, it did not feel good being the object of the perpetrator's behavior. Indirect aggression is difficult to explain and to express to others but do not be fooled, it is real and more prevalent among black women. Research has proven females both young and old preferentially use indirect aggression. Some scholars suggest indirect aggression increases with age. It is my desire that this book will educate both the perpetrator and the victim on the effects of indirect aggression. If you are the perpetrator, it is my prayer you will become more conscious of your behavior coupled with the desire to change. If you are the victim, I pray you will gain insight on how to address this issue without falling prey to it. In most cases, you did not do anything wrong. You are the victim of someone else's circumstances, anger, experiences, and low self-esteem. It is also my desire that *Cultural Shock* will create a desire in women to build healthy and productive relationships with other women. No, it may not be easy or free of conflicts, but I believe alliances can surface in the midst of conflicts.

I am a firm believer that we can build long lasting meaningful relationships that are valuable and productive to our organizations, churches, families, and communities. My sisters, I remain hopeful that one day we will walk in the footsteps of our ancestors; Betty Shabazz, Coretta Scott King, Dr. Margaret

Burroughs, and Madame C. J. Walker. They were able to push pass the aggression and place differences aside in order to leave a legacy for our generation. It is my prayer that we are able to do the same for the next generation and the generations to come. Until then, I remain hopeful.

Dr. Katrina L. Sweet

CONTENTS

Acknowledgements

First, I would like to acknowledge and thank God, my Heavenly Father. It is because of Him that I live, move, and have my being! None of this would be possible without Him. Since my last book, *"Silent Screams From Within: A Woman's Story From Tragedy to Triumph"*, God has done exceedingly and abundantly above all I could ever ask or think. And guess what? God is not finished. The best is yet to come!

With heartfelt thanks, I would like to thank my children, Tashika and Kevin and my dear friends and sisters in Christ, Joan Lucas and Donna Kinard. Thank you for standing with me through the thick and thin and encouraging me to give birth to this baby when I wanted to abort the vision. You are wonderful, and I thank God for you every day. Love you all so very much!

I would also like to thank my Life Coach, Dr. Danny Ellis. Thank you for your prayers, encouragement, and the Godly wisdom you have poured into my life. Because of you, doors were opened and opportunities were offered that otherwise would not have happened had I not been connected to you. I am humbled and forever grateful. Again, thank you!

PREFACE

Dr. Katrina Sweet is the epitome of a woman who knows how to turn lemons into lemonade.

Throughout her life, when faced with challenges, disappointments, betrayal, and loss, her faith has strengthened her. She is resolute in turning her mess into a message, her test into a testimony, her trial into triumph, and victim into victory.

I have known Dr. Sweet for over fourteen years, where we met at the Church we both attended. As a new Mom, I was very peculiar who cared for my child in the nursery. My fears rested when Dr. Sweet – (Katrina back then), worked in the nursery. She loves children, and her work and mission over the years have reflected that. As a mother herself, of two lovely children, she knows and has demonstrated first hand, the love, nurturing, discipline and guidance children need to grow holistically. She is an advocate for the welfare of children in the community, schools and churches. Dr. Sweet goes head on in addressing issues like bullying, literacy, and child protection, through workshops and advocacy groups by educating, empowering, and bringing awareness to children welfare.

She appears smooth, like velvet, and sometimes unassuming, but beneath is a strong, tenacious, resilient confident woman. Thus, it comes as no surprise, that her latest book "Culture Shock" is a Best Seller. It is a "must read" for all professionals, entrepreneurs, educators, employers, employees, wives, mothers, churches, and every organization.

The riveting truth of "Indirect Aggression" which Dr. Sweet has tackled is alive and this book is a "must read". Many have been directly or indirectly affected by it and its poisonous venom was dealt with in this book.

Congratulations on your mission Dr. Sweet as you educate, empower, and force us to do introspection and take positive actions in our lives to relate with our fellowman! Eyes have not seen, and ears have not heard the things that God has planned for you.

I am proud of you! I Love you!

Mrs. Donna Kinard, BSN, LNC, RNA, Entrepreneur

FOREWORD

Wow, what an excellent read. Dr. Katrina Sweet employs a unique writing technique that makes *Culture Shock* instructive, inspirational, and illuminating. It is obvious throughout of the personal dichotomy that exists between her professional assessment and her personal pride as a woman. *Culture Shock* delves deeper into the concept of indirect aggression introduced in my book called *"Why Men Don't Come Home After Five."* Instead of merely mentioning the un-comfortableness associated with this practice, Dr. Sweet peels back the pain and prognosis of both the perpetrator and the target.

Indirect aggression is misunderstood and grossly under studied. It has left its footprint in work places, professional organizations, churches, and even households. Whether intentional or not, it has resulted in the complete demise of trust between women who are already at a financial and promotional disadvantage. Historically, women have waited patiently while being more than qualified comparative to their male counterparts for the next promotion only to have it later snatched away because of an unnecessary catfight. Dr. Sweet has both researched and experienced the impact of this destructive behavior.

Culture Shock challenges every reader to move from a philosophical praxis to actual practical perusing by offering real life scenarios begging for analysis. *Culture Shock* spends very little time with unnecessary dissecting of the etiology of the culprit but spends efficient time revealing its devastating outcome. However, Dr. Sweet as a seasoned researcher does take the time to suggest that the Power Dead Even Rule is the motivation behind this subconscious behavior. Women just want to be equal. The irony is that indirect aggression not only fails to make women equal but actually results in a further loss of equity in all relationships and realms.

It would be easy for *Culture Shock* to have ended with exposing the childish catfights often surfacing just to either get the attention of a male supervisor or eliminate the possibility of a promotion by ruining the reputation of a well deserving woman. However, *Culture Shock* offers some strong feasible recommendations worthy of careful consideration. All places, all gatherings, and all relationships are better when trust flows freely. *Culture Shock* begins the door opening process. The fact that you are reading this book means that you are already apart of the solution. Bravo Dr. Sweet: Your pride as a woman is evident.

Dr. Danny Ellis
Ellis Research & Consulting Service, LLC

INTRODUCTION

One Sunday morning as I sat in church, I reminisced about the previous week at work and honestly, I was dreading the upcoming week. This should have been the highlight of my career. A recipient of a PhD in Organization and Management, doors of opportunities were opening. As an Adjunct Professor, Motivational Speaker, and the opportunity to work with God's most precious gift to this world, children, I was finally walking in my purpose. However, at the same time, I begin to experience resistance, controversy, and attacks from other women. This became more obvious while training for one of my new positions. The supervisor thought it was a good idea to familiarize myself with the operation of the organization before staff returned. He made arrangements with an employee to show me the internal workings of the organization. The young lady that trained me by no means said anything out of the way to me. She came across as extremely nice. She spent most of her time trying to gather information from me about my personal life and I must admit that struck me as odd. I learned very early in life that you never confide in or share secrets about your personal life or anything else with women you work with. Although confiding can build relationships and bring you closer together, the potential of indirect aggression surfacing makes it problematic. If power shifts in your favor, you become vulnerable to her exposing the information you shared with her. Since I was aware of the danger of making friends at work, I have always been cautious about women who did otherwise. Besides, I knew her ultimate goal was to gain a better understanding of my connection to our supervisor. She wanted to know why he chose me over the other candidates. The fact that I had a PhD and was a former educator did not matter to her. All she knew was I was a black female invading her turf. If the truth be told, if you would have placed my curriculum vitae against any of the other candidates that applied for the job, you too, would have chosen me.

At the end of the training, an unexpected feeling of devastation gloomed over me. Somehow I knew trouble was lurking around the corner. As I prepared to exit the building, her nonverbal disposition screamed, "I am going to do everything to make sure you do not succeed or outshine me at this organization". My thought process was totally different. I was excited about working together as a team to achieve the objectives of the organization. Not one time did the word, "competitor" ever cross my mind. I am comfortable in my own skin and do not find competing a necessary tactic when achieving goals. Shortly thereafter, she began to undermine, compete, and display elusive behavior towards me. I did not mention this to my supervisor. I feared being labeled as a "troublemaker". He was a male, and I was not sure if he would have understood or if I could have even explained it to him. Most males view this behavior as "petty or as "catfights". Catfights often occur among women in various settings. Although most women deny it, the inconvertible truth about women still stands. When women work together there is a greater potential for catfights or clashing. Catfights are described as spreading rumors, malicious gossip, divulging secrets, and attacking one another in the presence of others, particularly the boss. It is a real nightmare for any leader. It creates division within an organization, destroys trust, and undermines the organization's endeavors.

Indirect aggression is hard to detect, describe, or explain to others. It is defined as an attempt to hurt another without obvious face to face conflict. In other words it is a form of aggression in which a perpetrator attempts to harm the target while trying to obscure their intent (Ellis, 2014). Most women prefer to use indirect aggression because this form of aggression increases the harm inflicted on the victim while minimizing the personal danger involve (Björkqvist, 1994). There is low risk to the perpetrator as she remains anonymous avoiding counterattacks and detection. The perpetrator attacks from behind, rarely to your face. If confronted, they will hide and act as if they done nothing wrong (Heim, Murphy, & Golant, 2003). In an effort to build allies, the perpetrator will talk negatively about you to others but then behave as if they are your friend. In its simplest form, it is subtle and the underlying factor is normally jealously. The perpetrator's ultimate goal is elimination. I am not proclaiming to know everything about indirect aggression. However, my job as a researcher is to research it, understand it, and build upon the scientific research that exists, while offering strong recommendations and practical strategies.

The title of this book was given to me as I sat in Church one Sunday morning. My plight in life landed me a position at a predominately black organization, and I supervised predominately black women. There was a lot of hostility, back biting, and manipulation among my subordinates. I kept thinking that we were all sisters. It was my belief that if anyone should be willing to work and stick together, it would be black women. I had witnessed disagreements in the workplace among black women, but never to this magnitude. Yes, I am a black woman but this particular Sunday morning, I realized you can be of the same ethnicity group, yet so different. At that moment, I experienced a "Cultural Shock".

As I researched this topic, I gained a better understanding. I realized that black women have displayed this behavior for years. Mothers display it toward daughters, sisters toward sisters, friends toward friends, supervisors toward subordinates, church members toward church members, and co-workers toward co-workers. This is no nuance. This behavior has existed for centuries. I believe if we searched the Bible, we would probably find behavior that reflects indirect aggression among women.

I am sure there are numerous reasons why indirect aggression exists among black women; however, it is not excusable. Women, we must hold each other accountable for our actions. *Cultural Shock* does just that, hold women accountable. In this book, I will share the experiences of both the culprit and victims of indirect aggression with the hopes of bringing awareness and deterring this behavior so we can build effective relationships in every area of our lives.

CHAPTER 1

The Power Dead Even Rule

The Power Dead Even Rule explains the complex behavior and relationships women have with each other. It is an invisible rule that operates behind the scenes that shapes our interactions with other women. It also explains the connection between power and self-esteem. These connections are the underlying factor of indirect aggression. In order for women to forge positive relationships, their power and self-esteem must be kept "dead even". It must be similar in weight and it must be balanced. Unbalanced power and self-esteem offset the equilibrium of the relationship. This makes the environment ripe for conflict to emerge.

Women are more comfortable with a woman that downplays her importance, accomplishments, and power. They are most uncomfortable with a woman that does not, and they refuse to support her in anyway. Most women have to downplay their accomplishments and power in order to make other women comfortable. Ironically, when a woman's power is moderated such as, she fails publicly, she goes through divorce, she loses her job, or she fails in school, she will find that other women are extremely supportive. By contrast, when a woman is doing well in life, she will find her inner circle to be extremely small, with little to no support. Why is this so? She is perceived to have more power than other women, and she appears to be confident in her abilities. This also makes the environment ripe for conflict and war.

Memory Lane # 1

A couple of years ago, my department and I were preparing for a state audit. We spent countless hours making sure the organization passed the audit successfully. Weeks before the auditor arrived, several reports were due to the auditor. Although I worked with other leaders in the department prior to the audit, on the day of the audit, the state auditor, my boss, another female co-worker, and I were the only ones present. As we sat around the table, the state auditor praised me because of the detailed and well written report she received. Big mistake! The auditor praised me in front of my boss and the female co-worker. This changed the entire atmosphere in the room. It was no secret, my co-worker's entire disposition changed. Why? The auditor praised me in front of the boss. In her mind, the Power Dead Even Rule was violated. When women perceive that another woman has more power, a greater self-esteem, or is praised by others, this creates an environment for conflict and war. It is at this point, catfights, rumors, attitudes, withholding of friendship, undermining, and gossiping will begin.

Women have been taught to use forms of indirect aggression when they are upset or want to convey a message to someone nonverbally. Young girls exemplify this behavior at a young age and this behavior tends to spill over into adulthood. When girls and women aggress against others, they almost invariably use indirect aggression (Vaillancourt, 2013). As women, when we sense the Power Dead Even Rule has been violated, instead of confronting a woman, we use invisible attacks to even the battle field. In the aggressors mind, indirect aggression maintains their power and self-esteem. As long as there is harmony and balance in the relationship, everything will be fine. Their power and self-esteem must be equal. In this case, the relationship is considered balance. It is only at this point a good working professional and personal relationship can occur. When the relationship becomes disproportionate, usually it is perceived that one woman increased her external power, while the other woman remained the same. There is no interpersonal equilibrium and the relationship is no longer balanced, at least in the mind of the aggressor. I have found that whatever the internal state of the aggressor is at that time, determines the outcome of the relationship. Normally this breeds discontentment and is bound to create trouble for the relationship. The aggressor scratches at the fact that another woman seems to have more power than she does. Remember, the power must be kept dead even. Whenever the Power Dead Even Rule has been violated, conflict always occurs.

Memory Lane # 2

I am a survivor of sexual abuse and bullying; therefore, I am always looking for ways to decrease violence.

Recently, I had the opportunity to work with youth at a very prominent organization. It was brought to my attention that bullying was an issue in the classroom on a daily basis. Since a bullying policy was already in place, I referred to the policy for direction. Although the policy was great, I thought a bullying prevention program along with the existing policy would address the bullying issues. The program did not require that the existing policy be "tossed aside" or "disregarded", only slight modifications were needed. My background includes implementing preventive measures that reduce violence in the workplace. Prior to working with this organization, I worked at a maximum security female prison. One of my job duties was addressing sexual assault. As a first time responder and a PREA (Prison Rape Elimination Act) Counselor, my primary focus was reducing sexual assault in prison.

I discussed the prevention plan with my supervisor and without hesitation, he gave me his support. A team meeting was called to discuss strategies of addressing bullying. Whenever there was a meeting, it was a custom to document and maintain a copy of the minutes for internal and auditing purposes. Within the minutes, I described the new bullying intervention program and the changes that would occur with the existing policy. I would always place a copy of the minutes in the organization's policy manual and leave a copy with the administrative assistant for the Executive Director. At this point, I was not concerned about who had written the existing policy. The organization had been in existence for a number of years and several employees had come and gone. One night, I received a telephone call from a female co-worker. She wanted to let me know that she had written the bullying policy several years ago and had already included all of the valuable information that was needed to support the vision and mission of the organization. I was a little caught off guard by the nature of the call and decided not to respond to it negatively. I remained focused on the issues at hand, designing and implementing a bullying prevention program so the students could be in a safe environment conducive to learning.

Once the program was designed and staff was identified to assist with the program, another meeting was called with staff. The program was outlined and staff had a clear understanding of how the program would operate. As usual, minutes were generated and a copy was placed in the organization's policy manual and given to the administrative assistant for the Executive Director. At this point, no modifications were made to the existing policy. Shortly thereafter, I received this email:

> *Hello Dr. Sweet,*
> *Please place the attached policies in the organization's policy manual; there were some grammatical errors corrected and a few minor changes or add-ins...thanks*

My first thought was this policy had been in place for several years. My second thought was why are you in the office at 9:30 p.m. reviewing the bullying policy. My third thought was why are you just now noticing the grammatical errors. My fourth thought was why are you making minor changes or add-ins? It was clear to me, after she read the minutes I left for the Executive Director, she assumed I had made changes to the existing policy. In fact, she was so sure she was in the office at 9:30 p.m. reviewing the bullying policy. Once she discovered I had not made any changes to the policy, that should have at least quenched her rage, right? No! In her mind, I had increased in external power because I designed and implemented the bullying prevention program, and she had remained the same. Since the relationship was no longer balance, she had to bring equilibrium back to the professional relationship by balancing power. Her way of balancing power was making modification to the existing bullying policy. She had to show me that she had just as much power to modify the bullying policy as I did. This is another example that the Power Dead Even Rule must maintain balance.

Memory Lane # 3

On March 1, 2013, I received an email from a woman I had met several months ago. In the subject area the letters were typed in bold caps: **THANK GOD FOR HAVING MY BACK!** When the enemy wants to destroy your self-esteem, he knows how to use broken people to do it. Portions of her email will be shared in various chapters of this book as I seek to uncover and reveal examples of indirect aggression and passive aggressive behavior. Although I am not a psychologist, it is my belief that some women suffer from both indirect and passive aggression. Passive aggression is defined as a deliberate and masked way of expressing covert feelings of anger. This involves a variety of behaviors designed to get back at another person without the other recognizing the underlying anger (Ellis, 2014). Let's start with a portion of the email and then I will conclude with the chronological events that led up to this email. For the sake of confidentiality, I will call her Monica. *(No modification was made to Monica's email. Grammatical errors and misspelled words will be found throughout her email).*

LIKE MY HUSBAND SAID YOU HELP HER SELL BOOKS, APPRANTLY NO ONE IS READING, CAUSE IF SO, THEY WOULD HAVE KNOWN WHO SHE IS WHEN YOU SAY HER NAME. SHE SHOULD HAVE TAKEN YOU AND EVERYONE OUT TO BREAKFAST. SHE MADE SOME MONEY, YALL FED HER AND SHE BOUNCED!! I WASN'T THE ONLY ONE IN THE GROUP WHO NOTICE THAT TOO. THEY SAID SHE SHOULD HAD FEDD ALL OF US (LOL) BUT'S THAT'S OK HOPEFULLY THE CHILDREN SHE SPOKE ABOUT GET IT!! IT APPEARS AND IT'S SHOWING NOW, YOU ARE GREEDY, SELF-CENTERED AND WANT TO USE PEOPLE TO PROMOTE YOURSELF. I LISTEN TO YOU IN THE MEETING SATURDAY AND I SAID WOW THAT GIRL CAN SELL SNAKE OIL… MY HUBBY IS STILL CONCERENED I SHARED SO MUCH WITH YOU ABOUT OUR FAMILY. BUT

TOO LATE I TOLD HIM THE DEVIL CAUGHT ME SLEEPING AND TRICKED ME AND I TALK TALK, YOU KNOW SATAN GETS YOU WHEN YOU ARE WEAK... I SAID I DON'T CARE WHAT SHE DEVULGE, IT'S OK ALL FAMILIE HAVE ISSUES.

I'VE KNOWN, EVERYONE I INTRODUCED TO YOU FOR YEARS, SO THEY KNOW ME INSIDE AND OUT, THEY DON'T KNOW YOU, ONLY AS "MY" FRIEND. SO I WILL WARN THEM. I DON'T CARE ABOUT WHAT YOU JOIN; I JUST WANT TO WARN THEM, SO IF THE DEVIL STARTS REVEALING DRAMA & FOOLISHNESS, THEY'LL KNOW. SO FINALLY, HERE'S MY DECISION, I WANT NOTHING TO DO WITH YOU AT ALL!!! I DON'T WANT YOU TO CALL, TXT/EMAIL ME AT ALL. I WILL DELETE YOU FROM MY LIFE, THEN PRAY FOR YOU AND BE DONE. I CAN'T STOP YOU FROM COMING TO WHAT I INVOLVED YOU IN, THAT'S MY FAULT, I SHOULDN'T HAVE.

MY HUSBAND REMINDED ME THAT YOU WANTED TO USE ME BECAUSE OF MY POPULARITY AND CONNECTIONS AND IT HAD STARTED TO WORK. MY CIRCLE KNEW NOTHING OF KATRINA SWEET, THEY HAD TO GOOGLE YOU BOO, IT WAS ME WHO DID WHAT I DON'T NORMALLY DO BRING SISTAS

IN MY CIRCLE OR AFFLIATIONS. I THOUGHT YOU WERE AN ABUSED PERSON THAT NEEDED LOVE.

I NORMALLY WATCH OUT FOR WOMEN LIKE YOU, ESPECIALLY ONE THAT COMES ACROSS ABUSED TO SEEK PITY TO GAIN SYMPATHY. AS A MATTER OF FACT I DO REMEMBER (WHICH I WAS GOING TO TELL YOU IF I HAD SEEN YOU SATURDAY), I WAS AT A SOCIAL GATHERING, AND I MENTIONED YOUR BOOK TO SOME OF OUR CIRCLE OF FRIENDS AND ENCOURAGED THEM TO READ YOUR BOOK. SOMEONE WHO KNEW YOUR FOLKS SAID KATRINA IS A BIG LIAR. THERE ARE TWO SIDES TO EVERY STORY, SHE JUST TOLD HER STORY. MY HUSBAND LOOKED AT ME AND SAID, SEE, LEAVE HER ALONE AND MOVE ON! I PRAY YOU WELL. I PRAY YOU SUCCESS, AND I WISH NOTHING BUT TRUE BLESSINGS AND GRACE.

Really? Did she really wish me nothing but true blessings and grace? On one hand, she wishes me nothing but success; Passive. On the other hand, I am a liar and was never abused; Aggressive. I was sexually abused by my stepfather from the age of 11 to 15 and by my pastor as an adult. Her remarks remind me of why victims of abuse suffer in silence. They fear not being heard and that others will not believe them. My concern was not if Monica or her husband believed me, that was irrelevant. There was something much deeper eating away at their conscious.

In 2011, I released my first book, an autobiography about my life and overcoming sexual abuse as a child. Incredible doors were opening and people were coming forward who were silent for years. I decided to contact several churches in the local area that had bookstores to see if they would be willing to sell my book. A relatively large church responded and agreed to sell my books. A consignment agreement was signed and sure enough, the books sold like hotcakes.

Several weeks later, I received an email from this young lady. She shared how blessed she was by reading my book. Although she had never been sexually abused she had recently discovered someone close to her had been the victim of sexual abuse. She expressed her interest in meeting me, and I eagerly agreed. Finally, I am walking in my purpose. I can now share with others the secrets of walking in freedom and help others who may have been victims of abuse. We met at a local restaurant and chatted for hours. She thought it would be a good idea to introduce me to a professional networking group she was a part of. The president of the group decided to invite me as the keynote speaker during one of their weekly meetings. Prior to the meeting, the president sent my bio as an introductory to the group. My bio included some of my accomplishments, including my educational attainments. To my surprise, I begin to see the first warning signs of conflict.

The day of the event was a success. I shared what God had given me to share and the other ladies were very warm and receptive of my message and me. Although Monica introduced me to the group, she was unresponsive and somewhat unenthusiastic about her friends' response to me. It was almost as if she had an issue with them embracing me and inviting me into their circle. I was too caught up in the moment to give it a lot of thought and decided not to give much energy or attention to the matter. I figured if her behavior was not a figment of my imagination, something else would surface. It did not take long for that proclamation to come to pass!

Most women do not want to see you do well, they just say they do. Most women have a "crab mentality". This concept is an interesting phenomenon that occurs in buckets of crabs. When one crab attempts to escape from a bucket of live crabs, the other crabs will pull it back down rather than allowing it to get free. At times the crabs seem almost malicious, waiting until the crab has almost escaped before pulling it back into the bucket.

The crab mentality is used to describe a kind of selfish and short-sighted thinking, "if I can't have it, neither can you." This term refers to individuals that pull other people down, denigrating them rather than letting them get ahead or pursue their dreams. When a woman has a crab mentality, she is not willing to allow another woman to get out of a situation or to get ahead. A woman who has found her purpose and attempts to pursue her dreams is often foiled by other women who attempt to hinder her progress. As a general rule, the accusation of having this type of mentality is a poor reflection of one's self-image.

Up until this point, Monica was the only black female in the professional networking group. She was the golden child, the one the group held in high regards. When she noticed their responses to me, she knew she would have to share the "spotlight" with me. It would no longer be all about her. At that moment, she no longer saw me as an ally but as a competitor. I knew then that I had to make a clean break from the relationship. Perhaps I should have communicated my concerns with her; however, it is very difficult to communicate with someone that views you as a competitor. Instead of communicating with her to resolve the conflict, I attempted to avoid her. The avoiding conflict means you fail to pursue your own concerns as well as those of the person with whom you are in conflict with (Heim, et al., 2003). I neither addressed nor resolved the conflict but went into hiding. My response to her behavior angered her and as a result, I received a harsh email filled with attacks, lashes, and innuendos.

Monica did not stop with the email. She held true to her word. In an attempt to build allies, she spoke negatively about me to others in the group. Once again, the Power Dead Even Rule had been called into play. Monica was outraged that the women connected with me so well. Because she refused to be honest about the underlying problem (her insecurities), her indirect aggression behavior emerged in the form of "gossip" about me to the other women in the group. Monica's payoff, the president decided it was best if I did not become a member of their group. Sounds like elimination to me! It is all a part of indirect aggression.

I found it interesting that Monica allowed her husband to convince her that she had something to do with my discovery and success. According to her husband it was her popularity that elevated me. No one was reading my book until she told them about me. She introduced me to about 25 women, so now she is responsible for my success? Yeah Right! Prior to meeting Monica, I was nearing the end of my PhD program. I was invited to have several book signings at various organizations. I was the keynote speaker for various functions, and I presented on both local and national levels. Oh, did I mention the 700 club (Pat Roberson) did an inclusive interview of me and aired my story on their program? Yet Monica believed she had something to do with my sudden discovery and success. Interesting concept, don't you agree? What's even more interesting is she really thought I cared that she decided to end the relationship. I had made that decision long before she ever sent me that email. She did not know it but sending me the email was the best thing she could have ever done for me.

Monica mentioned her husband several times in the email. When I read her email, I could not help but wonder why her husband had so much to say about me. He had never met me. I asked myself over and over again, "Why does he appear to be so angry with me?" Sometimes we can remind people of what they did or failed to do. Remember what drew Monica to me was my story of sexual abuse. She had recently discovered that a close family member was sexually abused. It was alleged the perpetrator was her husband's brother. Like most families, it was the best kept secret. It is my belief that Monica's husband was afraid that I would somehow convince her to tell the family's secret. He saw me as a threat, and he needed to find a way to discredit me and eventually eliminate me. I was not at all upset that she decided to end the friendship. She did exactly what I wanted her to do. However, I would be lying if I told you I was not hurt by her malicious and vicious attacks. Her behavior was a classic sign of indirect aggression. This was necessary and indeed a lesson learned. Up until this point, I was naïve and optimistic about people. The truth of the matter is people are who they are. Maya Angelou once said, "When people show you who they are, believe them."

Sisters, resist the urge of sending an email of this nature to anyone. Emails are easy to trace and once you click the send button, you cannot retrieve it. It now becomes public knowledge and you cannot control how the intended target will use the email. My advice to you is to treat every email as though it was open to the public to read. Don't say things you don't want others to read, and remember that even after you've deleted your emails, they will be available for years from other sources. I know you think you are being direct, but you are actually being indirect. Attacking me via email instead of facing me was a cowardly move but just like anything else, I picked myself up by the boot straps, dusted myself off, and continued to press forward. My purpose in life was much bigger than Monica or her husband. It was so sad they had convinced themselves otherwise.

CHAPTER 2

Are All Women Equal?

Most women seek ways to keep things equal in their relationships with other women. While comparing themselves to other females, they look for ways to downplay another woman's accomplishments or her physicality. They are constantly seeking for signs or evidence that emphasize they are just like the woman who has accomplished a lot. I submit to you that women may share similar characteristics, similar backgrounds, similar experiences, and similar stories but they are not equal. I believe everyone has value, but not everyone is equal.

After I published my first book, many women that had been victims of sexual abuse really thought because we shared a similar experience, we had more in common than we actually did. The person they were reading about in the book was not the same woman that stood before them. I do not look or behave as a victim of sexual abuse. Once they realized there was no residual of the abuse, which would make us equal, they sought other ways to bring equilibrium to the relationship. Sometimes, this emerged in the form of indirect aggression. I supposed if I allowed life or my past experience to get the best of me, the need to balance power would not be necessary. Women try so hard to diminish or downplay who you are or what you have accomplished in order to maintain balance. Once they see that they cannot accomplish that mission, they find other tactics.

Memory Lane # 4

Recently, my organization hosted our first black tie gala event in the community. The purpose of the gala was to give a scholarship to a high school senior and to honor community leaders. It was also a strategic approach to introduce the community to our organization. I was not surprised when I entered the building and saw women that did not like me and had expressed their behavior in the form of indirect aggression. Did they attend the gala to be supportive? Of course not! They were inquisitive and curious. If the event was successful, they wanted to know if they were able to pull off such an event. If the event was not successful, they wanted something to talk about. Never forget, everyone wants power chips in the game. The event was a huge success. From the live entertainment to the keynote speaker, everything flowed seamlessly.

I was humbled that God allowed my first event to be a success. Everything I had was riding on the success of the event. Some women attempted to leverage their power chips in the game. Women are often "sisters in sadness". Women provide support when times are hard or when there appears to be signs of trouble. But what happens when something good happens, like a successful event or a job promotion? I can tell you this, several women's demeanor changed after the black tie gala. One woman in particular, her behavior was more obvious than others. A couple of days after the black tie gala, we were at one of the local churches. It was interesting that she withheld a simple hello. In order to leverage the power chips, she had to minimize my power chips by withholding communication. She tried to diminish my power by ignoring me, not speaking to me, refusing to make eye contact with me, and refusing to acknowledge my existence. This gave her the internal power she needed to balance her chips and bring balance back to the equation. Every woman keeps a chip bank account on other women. Sometimes there is a deficit in their chip account that is often beyond your control. Some women are actually upset that you are successful, beautiful, wear nice clothes, drive a nice car, or the mere fact that the one available bachelor is no longer on the market because he chose you.

Rather than striking back, you must be strategic about your approach. Manage your demeanor by holding your head high and keeping all communication on a professional level. If you are experiencing indirect aggression from women on your job, focus on the mission and objectives of the organization. Be careful not to complain about her to others, especially to other women. The first chance they get, they are going to tell her what you said. Women talk too much. In addition, be conscious about any facial expressions and body language when communicating or interacting with her. Subtle facial expressions can communicate unspoken feelings. Never let them draw you into their dark world or rob you of your dignity. You control the power chips by maintaining your dignity. Never part with it at any price or under any pressure.

Surviving in the game and keeping chips in the bank is essential. According to Heim et al. (2003), the Chip Theory is a sense of equity. The rule of the theory is to always maintain enough power chips in the bank to control the behavior of women that suffers from indirect aggression. Always take the high road. You cannot afford to create a chip deficit in your power bank. Remember, females who suffer from indirect aggression will always seek to make it even in the end. Stay focus and do not succumb to their personal attacks. The issues at hand are far bigger than they are.

Memory Lane # 5

I'M STILL PREPLEXED HOW A 3O + CHRISTIAN WOMAN ACT LIKE AN IMMATURE LIL GIRL, THAT GETS MAD AND GET A SERIOUS ATTITUDE, I WOULD HAD NEVER DONE THAT, BUT THEN AGAIN, EVEN THO I LOOK AS YOUNG AS A 30 YEAR OLD, I'M ALMOST 50. I HOPE YOU DO NOT ATTEND THE CLASS I TEACH AT THE YMCA, BUT THEN AGAIN, THAT CLASS IS FOR PEOPLE THAT ARE IN SHAPE. SO THAT PRETTY MUCH WILL TAKE CARE OF ITSELF!

Monica concluded that I was an immature Christian woman acting like an immature little girl. I was neither upset nor immature. I learned earlier that avoidance was better than confrontation. The avoiding conflict style allows you to tactfully side step the perpetrator and withdraw from a toxic relationship without causing further harm. Avoiding can be useful when the problem at hand is only a symptom of a larger issue. In this case, there were underlying factors behind Monica's explosiveness, and I was not prepared nor equipped to resolve the conflict with her at that time.

As you can see, the avoiding conflict style can cause small issues to intensify when you fail to address them. When we fail to confront issues, small issues have the tendency to escalate and have the potential to limit your success and productivity.

Monica had to find a way to even the chips in the game. She did what most women do, focused on her physical appearance. Yes, to be a 50 year old woman, she had the body of a 30 year old. I was never intimated by that because I brought more to the table than just my physical appearance. However, when all a woman brings to the table is her physical appearance, she tries to diminish or attack other women who may not be as attractive as she is, even though they have accomplished more. Likewise, less attractive women attack women that are more attractive and have accomplished more than they have accomplished. In 2013, I completed and graduated with a PhD in Organization Management. Women with a lower level of education refused to celebrate my educational accomplishment. However, they enrolled in school to obtain another degree. Now isn't that strange? If education was not all that important, then why were they in school trying to obtain another degree? I cannot tell you how many times I heard them say,

"Just because she has a PhD does not make her any better than me." No, obtaining a PhD does not make me any better than a woman who does not have a PhD but it certainly does not make me any less either. They found it hard to celebrate my PhD accomplishment but wanted me to run through troops to celebrate them. I learned very quickly to find solace in my own accomplishments. Looking to other women to celebrate who you are or what you have accomplished is not beneficial. Celebrating you causes a deficit in their power chip bank and that is too much of a price to pay. In the end, they want the equation to be equal rather than you being successful.

CHAPTER 3

The Elimination Process

Women operate from a point of scarcity and whenever this happens, they always try to find ways to eliminate anyone they view as a potential threat. Why does scarcity drive women wild? Scarcity drives women to action, causing them to act quickly out of fear of missing out on an opportunity or a potential relationship. Losing something before you had the opportunity to possess it drives women to action. The threat of loss creates a sense of urgency in a woman's actions or decision making. Women do not want to miss out on anything they could have had, whether it is an opportunity, a job, a promotion, or a man. Whenever their choices are limited or threatened, the need to maintain a share of the limited commodity makes a woman crave and latch on to that thing she fears will be limited or removed. Researchers call this behavior reactance (Rains, 2013). Reactance occurs when a person feels that someone or something is taking away their choice or limiting the range of alternatives. The idea of losing their freedom of choice sends them into a panic and attack mode.

When you are interacting with women that

operate from a point of scarcity, you can expect signs of indirect aggression and competition to surface. Women want what they want, and they want it at any cost. Competition among women is often indirect rather than direct. Competition can destroy relationships both personally and professionally. If women are not aware of this dynamic, it can create situations in which the Power Dead Even Rule is unconsciously violated.

Memory Lane # 6

Several years ago I worked at a large governmental organization. It should not surprise you the women ratio was greater than the male ratio in the department I worked in. This created issues between the women in the department. They were always competing for men, both married and unmarried. In a strange way, they always gravitated and competed for the men that were married. I noticed the rivalry and competition among the women made them vicious and nasty towards each other. There is no doubt indirect aggression is used in the context of competing for mates. If a woman had an eye or interest for a particular man, to discredit other women, she would bad-mouth her competition to him. They all desired to be the center of attention in the department, and they went through great lengths to make that happen. Often times this included self-promotion and derogation of their competitor.

According to Valliancourt (2013), self-promotion involves epigamic displays of physical attractiveness such as wearing make-up or provocative clothing to attract a potential male partner. Derogation involves a woman attempting to distort a potential male partner's perception of her competitor. This is done by being critical of the competitor's appearance or by spreading rumors that questions the trustworthiness or level of promiscuity of another woman. This type of competition was so distasteful to me I vowed to never be a part of such foolishness. One, I did not like what it did to other women, and I certainly did not like the tactics they used to attempt to eliminate other women. Competition can bring out the worst in women, simply because women are not taught how to compete without becoming personal in the battle.

Memory Lane # 7

Suzanne, a good friend of mine had landed a new job at a major corporation. Suzanne was attractive and smart. She had relocated to a new area and was excited about a fresh start in her career. After a couple of days of settling on the job, she was introduced to a young lady that happened to be a good friend of the president of the organization. Nothing more was said between the two women other than hello. A few days later Suzanne learned the young lady went to the president of the company and in an indirect way tried to taint her character. That was her first time ever meeting Suzanne. She wasted no time expressing what she heard about Suzanne to the president. After Suzanne told me what happened, I could not help but wonder if intrasexual competition played a role in this situation. Intrasexual competition is an effective approach that is used by women when they seek to eliminate a competitor. The fact that young girls and women use indirect aggression towards same sex peers is in keeping with the hypothesis that indirect aggression is used in the context of competing for mates (Valliancourt, 2013).

Suzanne relationship with the president of the organization was platonic. She had no personal interest in getting to know the president of the organization. Perhaps the president's friend had a secret desire and interest. Since Suzanne is an attractive young lady, she had to find a way to eliminate her by slandering her character. Females attack females on appearances and sexual fidelity because males value these qualities in women who are potential mates. Suzanne never said whether or not the president of the organization was interested in her but here is what I do know, if he was not, his friend was going to see to it that it stayed that way.

Indirect aggression serves it purpose when a woman is able to eliminate or reduce her rival's ability or desire to compete for a mate. Their behavior is normally camouflaged. This decreases the risk of detection and a counterattack. Although indirect aggression reduces the aggressor's risk, in many cases it does not go without detection. The derogation of a rival in the case of Suzanne and the president's friend carries the risk of calling men's attention to the rival thus increasing the number of competitors. This becomes nothing but a playground for men that are not looking for a commitment. In this case, everyone loses. Furthermore, it let men know you are not a nice woman, which may inadvertently reduce your chances of being with him. Men like nice women, not nasty or naughty women. Finally, it increases the chances for the intended target you meant to harm to confront you.

What God has for you is for you. You do not have to step over anyone, attack anyone, or try to eliminate anyone. When God opens a door for you, no one can shut it. Know this, karma is real, and when you try to shut doors for others, doors will not open for you.

CHAPTER 4

Real Live Scenarios

In the previous chapters, I shared with you my experiences of indirect aggression with the exception of Suzanne's experience. This chapter will provide real live scenarios of other women experiences in addition to the conflict styles and outcome of each scenario. It is my hope that this chapter will provide you some lead way of handling conflict with women who suffer from indirect aggression. Conflict occurs when the needs, wants, and likes of two individuals clash or appear to be incompatible. Women relationships are complex and there is an additional layer of intricacy that trouble women's relationships, especially as women try to matriculate through an organization or climb the ladder of success in both their personal and professional lives. If the truth be told, we all need to learn how to handle conflict and how to manage our power chips without the risk of becoming enmeshed in a conflict with women who in the big scheme of things, aren't really that important. In the book, *In the Company of Women, Pat Heim, Susan Murphy, and Susan Golant* outlined five conflict styles that are often used to resolve conflict; 1) Competing Conflict Style; 2) Collaborating Conflict

Style; 3) Avoiding Conflict Style; 4) Accommodating Conflict Style; and 5) Compromising Conflict Style. A woman's temperament and personal disposition will dictate which conflict style she is more than likely to gravitate towards.

Competing Conflict Style

Competing is an assertive and uncooperative conflict style. An individual that uses this style tends to try to win at all cost. He or she pursues their own concerns at the expense of others by using force, pulling rank, exerting coercive power, and arguing. Rarely are they willing to relinquish their goals for any reason. Negotiation is not an option.

Collaborating Conflict Style

Collaborating involves working with another person to find solutions that satisfies all parties involved. New methods of brainstorming maybe sought out as an alternative to finding creative solution in resolving conflicts. A collaborative approach preserves and strengthens relationships. It is a preferred conflict style for most women. However, this style can be time consuming as it requires too much time and energy in discussing issues that do not deserve a lot of attention. For instance, it is hard to collaborate with someone who only wants to compete with you.

Avoiding Conflict Style

This conflict style is the opposite of collaborating. An individual that uses this style fails to pursue their concerns as well as others. They neither address nor resolve a conflict but rather overlook it or go into hiding. In other words, they are viewed as side stepping a conflict or withdrawing from a threatening situation. In Chapter 1, I briefly mentioned this conflict style when describing my relationship with Monica. This was not the only time I had gravitated towards the avoiding conflict style. This style can be quite useful, especially when the relationship is vital and the conflict is petty. I have used this conflict style in relationships I valued and held in high esteem.

Accommodating Conflict Style

A person using this style is viewed as submissive and compliant. This style is the opposite of competing. He or she neglects their own need in order to satisfy the needs of others, even if they are in conflict with them. This includes an element of self-sacrifice, selflessness, or yielding to another's viewpoint in opposition to your own.

Compromising Conflict Style

This conflict style falls somewhere between competing and accommodating. The objective is to find a mutual solution that partially satisfies all parties involved. It is a form of sharing. Neither side dominates but instead, they seek to find common ground in agreement. No one gets everything they want, but each one is willing to give in for the sake of reaching a common goal in order to build trust and collaboration. Both parties are drawn to the bigger picture, understanding they will not get everything they want. However, they do believe they get something out of the deal and this is perceived as *"even"* which equates to the Power Dead Even Rule.

As we move forward, we will examine and work through various scenarios. We will also review the outcomes and conflict style used. You will have the opportunity to contribute to the discussion with each scenario.

Scenario # 1

I have been a professional who works in a male dominated work environment for over 20 years. It is somewhat difficult to recall a time where indirect aggression and /or passive aggressiveness was not the norm. Unfortunately, because this behavior is more the standard than not, my methods of dealing with it is unconsciously done. I have adopted methods of interaction, communication and processes that are a direct result of indirect aggression during the early parts of my career. Truthfully, I have been the recipient and the aggressor. Learned behavior works in both positive and negative ways.

When interacting with coworkers and subordinates this kind of behavior teaches you to avoid unnecessary interactions and people in general. You learn to make the job and its duties the primary motivator in everything you do at your place of business. You learn to have thick skin and high tolerance for exclusionary tactics used against you and used by you. It has been an evolutionary journey to now be conscious of these acts. I find that I may execute exclusion before it has been earned by my recipient. You also learn to value the mirror and value less of those who are actually around you. All of these issues results in your becoming numb to people in general. And for me, it was the professional motivator to becoming the best at what I do. Validation and inclusion would not come from these people, so validation was defined by promotions and inclusion was defined by me.

Specific experiences surrounding indirect aggression included gender, sexuality, race and faith. In each of these cases the motivating factor was more about my having a different and normally, a minority point of view. Simply put, I have the gift of gab and the gift of words so most people cannot out write me or out speak me. Thus, most people chose to utilize the only method left which was indirect aggression. This aggression materialized in the form of undermining decisions made or reverse tasks that were completed or blatantly filing erroneous or incomplete reports about my behavior. The examples are simply too numerous to recall but the feelings they evoked in each case, is crystal clear. Primarily I felt disappointment, anger, and disgust.

In my profession, there are many women who capitalize on being a woman. In both the professional world and personally, they may not execute because they know a man will come and handle it for them. Perhaps this is mostly a physical task but still very noticeable especially when the job assignment includes physically moving something from one place to another or going the extra physical mile. Even if they could do it themselves, my female coworkers, subordinates, and supervisor would play the "damsel" in distress or the physically inferior species to "entice" the male in the area to do it for them. I would not do this. It resulted in early respect from men that had no price tag attached to it and it was one of the reasons the aggression would begin. When it was against me, mysteriously all of the males were never available to me and most of my task for the day was physical. I had to make it on my own or admit that THEY needed to find someone to help me. And unfortunately when I became the decision maker I found myself making sure the males were unavailable to "help". I could show them better than I could explain.

Perhaps the most significant example for me involves sexuality. Since I have always been categorize as a very dominate woman and masculine in some of my mannerisms and attitude, I have always been left out of many social or interactive exchanges and not invited to the "outside" of business gathering. Usually because of the assumption that I was gay and clearly wanted every woman who was near me. Women who are not comfortable with themselves tend to fear interactions with me. Black women tend to "grin" in my face and speak ill behind my back. There was a meeting once where there were only two women in attendance; myself and another black woman. She spent the entire meeting overtly allying with one of the males and overtly going against every thought and idea I had. That meeting taught me to present ideas in the best way possible. It also taught me going against my idea would mean career suicide. Some may say I am arrogant and single minded but I am really confident and self-assured.

I can also recall another female that refused to be alone with me for more than 5 minutes. She feigned an illness so that she could be replaced as my partner in completing a task. Then she proceeded to illustrate to everyone how I was "looking" at her. The avoidance was overt by those who bought into her "story". Unfortunately, this exclusion via my sexuality has made me very leery to befriend women in general. I am overtly difficult to get to know on any level, even professionally. I keep women at a great distance from me because most let the fear of my possibly "liking" them influence how they interact with me. When someone's behavior is altered because of what might happen or my allowing my feelings to come to the surface, it is very hurtful when you are the recipient of that altered behavior. Therefore, I avoid the natural communion that women enjoy with each other. I don't befriend and I don't interact. I stand alone and I am lonely because of it. But I am alive and I am healthy and I can choose my world.

I have made significant achievements in my field through hard work and I have paved a pathway for women leaders and minority leaders by being the best at what I do and not forgetting the pathway that lead me to the opportunity to achieve. In spite of this achievement, women are the greatest challenge in accepting my commitment to providing opportunity, creating change and demanding professionalism as it relates to leadership in general. And more specifically, black women are the leaders in the perpetuation of indirect aggression. It seems that the old saying that references black people having a "crab" mentality is applicable and true, especially for black women. Simply put, if one sees another with an achievement, a relationship, or success of any kind they will do whatever it takes to pull the other from that opportunity. I try not to be motivated by anger or revenge but behavior is learned and taught. Life has given me some hard lessons and I am in the beginning of truly learning to monitor my own behavior to make sure that I am not doing what has been done to me. I know now to teach the lesson and not be the story.

Can you identify indirect aggression? If so, Explain

____

____

____

Conflict style used

____

____

____

Comments

____

____

____

Scenario #2

I had recently gone through a bad relationship and was trying to pick up the pieces in my life. As always, when you have hit rock bottom, women have a tendency to act as if they are your biggest supporters. For me, my biggest supporter appeared to be my cosmetologist. You know misery loves company! As long as I did not have anyone, she was right by my side but as soon as a young man started to show interest in me, things changed. He showered me with flowers, gifts, and attention. For my birthday, he knew I was getting my hair done and decided to send me flowers to the beauty shop. Unfortunately, I had already left when the flowers were delivered. My sweet dear cosmetologists refused to call me when the flowers were delivered. Instead, she felt the need to call the young man that sent me the flowers. Out of courteous, she wanted to let him know that I was married. She knew I was separated from my husband and so did he. She just did not know that he knew. Now here is the amazing thing, my cosmetologists was no saint, at the time, she was involved with a married man. She was so busy trying to block my happiness, she forgot to tell him she was involved with someone else's husband. Women have been dirty for a very long time. They are miserable and really do not want to see anyone else happy. I confronted her but of course she lied as most women do. Most women throw rocks but hide their hands. In the end, what did she really get out of it? Nothing! She lost me as a client, and she lost his respect because he saw her for who she really was. I learned at that moment to always be transparent and truthful when moving forward in a relationship. If not, manipulative and jealous hearted women will find a way to tell it.

Can you identify indirect aggression? Explain

____

____

____

Conflict style used

____

____

____

Comments

____

____

____

Scenario # 3

I was a happily married woman and never had any questions or doubts about my relationship with my husband. He treated me well and took great care of the kids and me. A co-worker that worked with my husband was extremely nice to my husband but was very nasty to me. I could not figure it out. She would be nice to everyone but me. I had never done anything to her. I could not understand her behavior towards me. She made it a point to speak and talk with everyone in the room but me. She overly communicated with my husband even when she did not have too. She wanted to flaunt her working relationship in my face for some reason. There was no prior history. I only saw her at community events or functions at my husband's job. My husband was in management, and she worked for him. She would even get upset if I was around. It appeared that my husband would try not to upset her if I was present, but it appeared my presence would upset her. If she got upset about my presence, he took his frustration out on me. I could live with her behavior because I understood that some women do not need a reason to be nasty or mean. What I could not understand was his behavior. He acted nervous and always kept his eyes on her to see what her next move was going to be. So, I decided to talk with my husband, and his response surprised me. He became irate that I questioned him. As a result of his response, I decided not to attend any of the company's functions because I did not like who he became in front of her. If she worked for him, why was he dancing to her music? Did she have something on him or was he having an affair with her? I never asked my husband any more questions about her. It's like the unspoken rule in our home. However, my heart is broken that it was never really resolved. His explanation made no sense to me nor did it satisfy me. I just cannot understand why my husband treated me differently in her presence. If I am his wife, why did he shun me when she was around? I was not the other woman, I was his wife. He did not want to upset her, but he did not care if I was upset. I love my husband and after I questioned him once, I never had a discussion with him again. I must tell you, it still hurts. I do not know if she still works at his organization or not. I felt that my marriage was important. I have three children and they need both parents. My way of dealing with it was staying away from the company. If she did not see me and I did not see her, then there would be no issues in my marriage.

I am not sure if I handled it the right way or not, but at least for now my kids have both their mother and father. And to me, that's all that matters.

Can you identify the indirect aggression? Explain

____

____

____

Conflict style used

____

____

____

Comments

____

____

____

Scenario # 4

In my department, I worked with majority women. This can be good and complicated at the same time. For the most part, I always got along with my co-workers. I enjoyed working together as a team and reaching the goals of the organization. This was not the mindset of everyone involved. One particular co-worker was promoted as lead supervisor of the department. I was happy for her because she had worked so hard for the promotion. Her immediate supervisor was not happy about the promotion because she had recommended someone else that happened to be a personal friend of hers. During departmental meetings, all lead supervisors would have to give a report of the department and current activities. Because her boss was not happy with her, she was always the last one to give her report. By this time, most people had left the meeting or people were tired and ready to go. My lead supervisor would always express to me that she felt rushed and that no one was really listening to her. She also believed her direct supervisor was treating her like that because she was upset that she was promoted over her friend. I suggested that she speak with her supervisor and express her concerns. A meeting was scheduled and she had the opportunity to express her concerns. Although the supervisor did not admit that she was deliberately treating her unfairly, she did discuss a previous incident she had not been able to let go of. After they talked, she decided to alternate the reporting schedule. My lead supervisor was willing to accept this since she would no longer be the last one to speak every single time. She felt that she was entitled to speak first for the remainder of the year since she had not had that opportunity to do so before; however, she was willing to accept the alternating schedule. In this case, both my supervisor and her immediate supervisor got something out of the deal.

Can you identify indirect aggression? Explain

____

____

____

Conflict style used

____

____

____

Comments

Scenario # 5

As a child, I was abused by an immediate family member. I always vowed to never be around the perpetrator as an adult. I never wanted my children to be around him either. My family could not understand why I felt this way or should I say they did not want to understand. Since I did not want to be around him during family gatherings and holidays, they excluded me all together. They would meet and not tell me they were meeting. They would plan vacations or go out on a family gathering, and I would always hear about it after the fact. Yes, my feelings were hurt. I could not understand why they were treating me like this. I wanted my family when he was not around. I wanted to be with my siblings but I did not want to choose. I was very clear about that so I guess they decided to choose. It did not take me long to realize that they chose him. In order to be with my family, I overlooked my needs and placed myself in an uncomfortable situation and my daughter in a dangerous situation. This would turn out to be the worst mistake of my life. When my daughter became of age, the perpetrator that abused me sexually abused my daughter also. Trying to please my family and go against what I knew was the best thing for my daughter and me only yielded the same results, another abused victim.

Can you identify indirect aggression? Explain

____

____

____

Conflict style used

____

____

____

Comments

____

____

____

CHAPTER 5

The Low-Self Esteem Syndrome

Meriam-Webster Dictionary defines self-esteem as a feeling of having respect for yourself and your abilities. Another definition defines self-esteem as confidence and satisfaction in oneself. More women suffer from low self-esteem than men. Partly because others often see women less self-confident than they actually feel they are. It is extremely difficult when a woman comes along and it appears she has high self-esteem to a woman who has low self-esteem.

Low self-esteem can damage and destroy relationships among women. Women with low self-esteem always try to balance power with a woman they perceive to have high self-esteem. According to the Power Dead Even Rule, low self-esteem coupled with reduced sense of power creates an imbalance in power. Relationships and how well you get along with other females will be determined by how well they think of themselves. For example, if you are highly confident in your abilities and feel good about yourself and she does not, this will more than likely create catfights in the relationship. Less secure women may feel envious of your self-confidence. They will perceive your confidence as too powerful and will try to destroy you and bring you down. In contrast, if her self-esteem is high and yours is not, it will skew the relationship and in a strange way, taint your view of her.

I believe there is a method to the madness. To balance and keep the balance in a relationship with another woman, you have the option of building up her self-esteem. Sincere compliments, support, and being understanding will help build her self-esteem because it enhances how she sees herself. Positive and supportive energy make a woman feel like she is worthy in your eyes. It is important that I share that even with this you have to be careful when focusing on enhancing her self-esteem. Since women are so vicious and scandalous, if they perceive you as too confident, they perceive you as powerful. If they perceive you as powerful, they may attack you because of how they perceive themselves. A wounded animal is more likely to attack you when you are trying to nurture or help them.

Memory Lane 8

At new hire orientation, I watched a woman break down and cry after she heard the boss shout accolades about my background and accomplishments. When the boss left, she continued to ask questions about my accomplishments. She wanted to know my plans of writing another book. She also wanted to know about my long term goals. As I answered her questions, she broke down and started to cry. Not knowing why she was crying, I allowed her to get herself together. As she gained her composure, she began to tell me her dream of having her own organization. Several of her colleagues have their own organizations, and she felt so far behind. I am a nurturing woman, so when she began to cry, it was a natural instinct for me to console her. As she cried in my arms, I shared with her that God would eventually give her the desires of her heart. I also shared with her that I am where I am because of God and if He did it for me; He will do it for her.

I thought I had showed her how nice I was and that I was a genuine woman. Instead it showed her that I was highly confident. The same woman that cried in my arms was the same woman that would stab me in my back. She spoke negatively of me, tried to minimize my accomplishments, and attempted to place me a box in order to soothe her own insecurities. She did not have a box big enough to place me in or small enough to contain me in. The road she was traveling, I had already traveled. So just know in most cases, there are repercussions in trying to console another woman and build her self-esteem.

There may or may not be a direct correlation between power and self-esteem. An individual with low self-esteem tends to act as if her power is greater than yours. In most cases, she overtly exerts what little power she has. If that does not work, she may try to build her power in covert ways like gossiping about a woman behind her back, disparaging her to her superiors, and downplaying her accomplishments to others. On the other hand, a person with high self-esteem does not have to do that in order to feel good about who she is as an individual. She does not need to become involve with such power games to prove how important she is.

Memory Lane 9

One day I was working on a major assignment for an organization. I always thought it was a good idea to keep the president of the company abreast about any activities or meetings that were going to be held at his organization. When I finished compiling the data and memos, I made a copy and placed it in the president's box. The administrative assistant removed the documents from his box and quickly walked into my office. She proceeded to tell me that it was best to submit this information after the activities had taken place. She gave the information back to me and walked out of the office. I placed the information in the president's box so why would she automatically assume the information was for her? I understand it was her custom to check his box and place all documents on his desk, but it struck me as odd that she felt she had enough power to consider herself equal to him. I gathered the documents and placed the documents back in his box. I informed her that the information was for the president and I wanted to inform him of the activities before they took place. Without warning, she snatched the documents from his box and abruptly placed the documents on his desk. Her behavior sent a clear message to me. She wanted to maintain her power chips. Early on in the relationship, she had shown poor signs of leadership and professionalism. Additionally, I knew she had been secretly trying to destroy me and my credibility behind my back. She wanted power and I refused to give it to her. I understood that when a woman's self-esteem is low, no matter how much power she obtains, you will have a difficult time building a solid professional working relationship with her. Since I knew this, I refused to become entangled in the web of deceit and confusion. It is very difficult to give someone power when you know someone is trying to destroy you or is seeking to diminish your power in order to amplify their own. It is difficult for women to understand that power flows to women through their relationships. No relationships, no power! Women with poor self-esteem find themselves in power- deficient situations. Unfortunately, this is problematic when trying to build relationships in both professional and personal settings. Most women with low self-esteem attempt to make themselves feel better by exerting the little power that they have, especially when they think those around them are constantly questioning their standing. As you can see, if a woman does not feel good about herself, she will more than likely start a "catfight" with her colleagues. This will help her feel good about herself. If a woman acts as if she is important and does not appear to lack in self-confidence, and you do not have the same perception of yourself, it will create ill feelings in you towards her. It is a no win situation and can create a hostile working environment for all parties involved.

CHAPTER 6

Women As Allies

I find it interesting that women can only come together when there is a common enemy. Over the years, I have observed the difficulty of women working together. They could only work together in unity when they are on a mission to destroy someone else. In my day to day observation, I noticed women who did not like each other became allies when there was a common enemy. If women can come together for a negative cause, then certainly they can come together for a positive cause.

Memory Lane # 10

Ann was an attractive young lady that started with an organization several months ago. Sarah, a young lady who had worked for the organization for several years did not accept Ann as a part of the team. Ann did not take it personal because it appeared that Sarah did not get along with the other co-workers. Ann did extremely well in her position. Months after joining the team, she was eventually promoted. The co-workers that had problems with Sarah started to dislike Ann also.

It was not long, her co-workers joined forces with Sarah. Controversy brought them together. It is so sad that the only time black women can come together is when there is some type of controversy or when there is a common enemy. Black women, we must do better.

Memory Lane # 11

Nicole was a prominent leader in her community. She had done so much for families and various churches in her community. She was well known and well liked. There were no debates or questions about her professional life. However, she went through some personal challenges that created a buzz within the community. She made decisions about her personal life, and some of the community leaders did not agree with her decisions. Her decisions created critics and enemies. They no longer saw her as a leader and wanted to have her removed from office. Nicole noticed that women that were enemies were all of a sudden friends. Prior to Nicole's personal dilemma, she tried to implement community projects that required team work and collaboration. According to Nicole, it was difficult to create teams because they saw each other as competitors and not collaborators. However, when she became arch enemy number one, they became allies. They would meet at each other homes for hours plotting and planning their next move. They were determined to destroy Nicole at all cost. It was easy for them to come together. They now had a common enemy. Think about what they could have done had they exercised their energy towards something positive.

How can we teach women to come together before controversy? With so much indirect aggression and competition, it is difficult to do so. This only brings credibility to the underlying factors of this book. Indirect aggression is real and so is competition. There is nothing creative about trying to destroy another person. The reason women can work so well together when they are trying to destroy someone else is because the element of creativity is not present. Women are creative creatures by nature but if you want to destroy creativity, fire up competition (Baer, Abhijeet, Lenders & Oldham, 2014). A study conducted at Washington University in St. Louis found that women can only join together when competition is not an option (Baer et al., 2014). This is a true indicator that when competition does not exist, women can work better together. That's why it is so easy for women to join together and become allies when they are seeking to destroy others. No one is competing. Everyone is on the same team with the same agenda. Ladies, we must do better. We must find a better way of coming together. Our families, children, churches, and communities are depending on it.

Instead of an enemy being the common denominator that brings you together, learn how to come together for the greater good. Learn to bring about change that will create opportunities for the next generation. I do believe that women can find a common ground, when they focus on something positive. We can learn a lot from each other if we can learn to be allies without the malicious intent to destroy someone else. In our connection, create an atmosphere that is positive and conducive to growth. If we want to change the stereotypes about us in society, we have to do something we have never done. Insanity is doing the same thing over and over again expecting a different result. Build positive relationships and find allegiance with encouraging and positive women. I believe then and only then we will discover that we can do things we never thought we would be able to do.

CHAPTER 7

Resolution

Please do not be discouraged. There is a method to the madness. I know it is difficult, but you can learn and survive through the process. One thing I learned, you can tell the story without becoming the story. I know this from personal experience. I wrote this book because of my personal experiences. The lessons I have learned over the last six months have been life changing, and I want to share them with you today.

1. Never become who they are. If you become who they are, you are showing them that indirect aggression works. Becoming who they are never resolves anything. It only makes matters worse. The vicious cycle continues. You must address the monster without becoming the monster (Ellis, 2014). Unless someone makes a conscious decision to be different, this behavior will continue. The cycle needs to be broken. Let it start with you.

2. Stay focused. Do not let others deter you from your purpose in life. Indirect aggression is nothing but a distraction. Their whole tactic is to eliminate you or stop you. Keep the main thing the main

thing and everything else should be secondary.

3. Remain professional and do not befriend them. Sometimes you have to leave people where they are. It is hard to be friends with someone that suffers from indirect aggression. Especially when they refuse to admit it. People that suffer from indirect aggression have low self-esteem. This is a clear sign that they are hurting in other areas of their lives. We make the mistake of trying to get close to and nurture someone that is wounded and end up getting hurt ourselves. Hurting people hurt others. Out of survival a wounded person will hurt you. Do you know what happens when you try to get close to a wounded animal? A wounded animal tends to act unpredictable and is known to be very dangerous. They have a flight or fight instinct. The flight and fight response is a response to an acute threat to survival that is marked by physical changes, including nervous endocrine changes, that prepare them to react or to retreat. It is an innate survival instinct, especially when they feel threatened. I recall when my neighbor's dog was chased by some of the neighborhood children. At first the dog decided to run (flight response) but once the dog was cornered, he decided to fight (bite) in order to stop the chasing once and for all. Although this is a lesson for women who try to befriend women that suffer from indirect aggression, it is also a lesson for the woman that suffers from indirect aggression. Eventually your victim becomes tired. She might flee or chose to ignore you at first, but sooner or later, she might attack you so your attacking her might stop once

and for all.

4. Surround yourself with positive people. There are still a few good people in this world that share the same sentiment as you. It is always refreshing to be in someone's presence that has the right spirit and the right attitude towards you. In your safe place, you can be you, share your feelings, and find comfort from those that love you. Make time to meet with this circle as often as time permits.

5. If the situation has escalated and you have to confront the aggressor, strategize your move. You need to be very strategic in your response. Confronting the aggressor can be beneficial to you, but it can also hurt you. People who suffer from indirect aggression do not like when you confront them. It makes them angry and extremely defensive. Familiarize yourself with the different conflict styles. Knowledge is power. Remember, some things sound good in theory but are not practical in reality. Every situation is different. There is no one size fit all approach. Find the best strategy, execute it, and continue to move forward. (Refer to Chapter 4).

6. If you are the aggressor, seek counseling. You may need to get to the root of your behavior. You cannot feel good about yourself knowing that you are secretly mistreating and trying to destroy others just to make yourself look good. You really need some help. Maybe once you seek counseling, you will discover the reasons why you behave the way you do. Second, stop acting like the victim. You are not the victim. You throw rocks and hide your hand and when you are exposed and/or

confronted, you become angry and play victim. The key to correcting your behavior is 1) admit you are wrong; 2) seek counseling; and 3) find someone you can be accountable to. They should remind you when you are displaying signs of indirect aggression. In addition, they should remind you of positive strategies to use to alter your behavior. It is time out for games. This behavior needs to stop.

I have discovered in the course of these six months that most women suffer from indirect aggression. Furthermore, I also learned that most women are not nice. They really do not want to see other women succeed in life. In the spirit of transparency, I struggled with writing this book. I do not like controversy. I knew this book made sense but it would not make friends. However, I knew if I did not write this book, I would be doing an injustice to the female population.

Recently, I was invited to attend a huge event at one of the local churches. I was the guest of one of the most available bachelor in our local area. After attending this event, any doubts I had about writing this book were erased. I knew I had to tell the story. Once the women both married and unmarried realized I was his date, indirect aggression surfaced. One woman made it her business to avoid me. She would not even make eye contact with me. She shunned me the entire night. I was not surprised by the reaction of the single ladies, but I was totally taken by surprise by the reaction of the married women.

Interestingly after the party, one of the women used social media to attack me. No, she did not call my name directly, but she had an awful lot to say about relationships and my Alma Mater, Capella University. People use social media to bully or be aggressive towards others. Social media is a tool they use to display their aggression. To me, they are cowards. They hide behind a computer screen while doing their dirty work. Is there a possibility her comments on Facebook was coincidental? More than likely not! Women are dirty and have been for a very long time.

Conclusion

So where do we go from here? I pray you are inspired and have a little more knowledge after reading this book. The real struggle is around change. Change is not easy but it is necessary. Mahatma Gandhi once said, "Be the change you want to see in the world." Ladies, if we want to see change, we must first become the change. If you are going to do anything that matters in life, you must strive to be a better person. Do not miss out on this opportunity. Your families are depending on it. Your communities are depending on it. I believe if we change our ways, we will experience life to the fullest. It is my desire that "Culture Shock" will give you the necessary tools that will launch you in the right direction.

Indirect aggression is a topic that is rarely discussed. Most people are not even familiar with the term which is the reason why I decided to write this book. I did not write this book out of anger. I wrote this book because I wanted to bring awareness to this topic, and I wanted to bring about change. I understand that most people are less likely to change and those that do, can experience a setback at any given time. During stressful times, people revert back to what they know. Nevertheless, I will continue to remain optimistic that people can and will change if they really want to.

For the women who were kind enough to read this book, please do not get defensive or bitter. My only intent was to help you, not harm you. After reading this book, what do you plan to do about indirect aggression? Well, if you are the perpetrator, you need to STOP IT! Indirect aggression at best is a mild form of bullying. It may seem that you are getting away with it, but in reality you are being set up for failure. Not only are you being set up for failure, but you are setting the next generation up for failure. If this behavior goes unchecked, it will lead to broken families, broken communities, failed relationships, and violent children. In the end, it will cost you more than you are willing to pay. The cycle will continue. Remember, children model what they see.

If you are the victim that has faced or are facing indirect aggression, try not to let it consume you. If you let it, it will consume your time and eventually your life. The underlying factor of indirect aggression is jealously. In a nutshell, the aggressor wants to be you. They spend their time studying you so they can imitate you. I know that this is scary, but you should find solace in the fact that you have achieved some level of excellence that someone wants to imitate you. Since they won't celebrate you, learn to celebrate yourself. If it becomes unbearable and you decide to address the monster, address the monster without becoming a monster in the process. In the midst of the process, it is important that you stay above it. You need to be strategic and methodical in your approach and actions. Nothing and no one is worth you losing out on what rightfully belongs to you. Stay focus and continue to move forward.

To all my senior managers, supervisors, leaders, husbands, and significant others, **yes**, indirect aggression is real. It is not a figment of their imagination. When brought to your attention, do not brush them off. I know it is difficult to relate to something you do not understand. Researching the topic for a better understanding is essential. In the end, it will dictate how you respond to it. Here are a few tips that may help you along the way. 1) Be willing to listen to her. Effective communication will help the victim and you through this process; 2) Be more observant. The behavior is subtle and hard to detect. The perpetrator tries hard to obscure their intent. If you blink, you might miss it; 3) Be decisive. At times, you may have to make a decision and confront the aggressor. No, you cannot control anyone's behavior. However, as leaders you must be willing to confront the controversy. You will find, some people won't stop until you confront them; and finally 4) Be supportive. Support goes a long ways. Your response to the victim and the situation is crucial. Every leader wants competent, capable, knowledgeable, and good people working for their organization. Every husband wants a good wife that loves, honor, and respects him. If you have been blessed to have that, learn to protect it. Good relationships both professional and personal are hard to find. If you have good people around you, learn to shield them from those who have a malicious intent because of their own selfish desires.

QUIZ

1. Define indirect aggression?

2. Define passive aggressive behavior?

3. Explain intrasexual competition among women.

4. (True/False) Indirect aggression is subtle and hard to detect. Explain your answer.

5. Describe the underlying factors of indirect aggression.

6. Do you believe indirect aggression is a learned behavior or genetic? Explain.

____

____

____

7. What conflict style describes your personality? Explain.

____

____

____

8. Despite the history between women, do you think women can build positive and effective relationships? Why or Why not?

____

____

____

9. Is indirect aggression a natural reaction for most women? Why or Why not?

____

____

____

10. Is it safe to assume that all black women are alike? Why or Why not?

____

____

____

THE AUTHOR'S FAVORITE POEM

By
Maya Angelou
You may write me down in history
With your bitter, twisted lies,
You may trod me in the very dirt
But still, like dust, I'll rise.

Does my sassiness upset you?
Why are you beset with gloom?
'Cause I walk like I've got oil wells
Pumping in my living room.

Just like moons and like suns,
With the certainty of tides,
Just like hopes springing high,
Still I'll rise.

Did you want to see me broken?
Bowed head and lowered eyes?
Shoulders falling down like teardrops,
Weakened by my soulful cries?

Does my haughtiness offend you?
Don't you take it awful hard

'Cause I laugh like I've got gold mines
Diggin' in my own backyard.

You may shoot me with your words,
You may cut me with your eyes,
You may kill me with your hatefulness,
But still, like air, I'll rise.

Does my sexiness upset you?
Does it come as a surprise
That I dance like I've got diamonds
At the meeting of my thighs?

Out of the huts of history's shame
I rise
Up from a past that's rooted in pain
I rise
I'm a black ocean, leaping and wide,
Welling and swelling I bear in the tide.

Leaving behind nights of terror and fear
I rise
Into a daybreak that's wondrously clear
I rise
Bringing the gifts that my ancestors gave,
I am the dream and the hope of the slave.
I rise
I rise
I rise.

My dear sisters, there is greatness in you. Tap into the greatness and be all that you were created to be. It is time to make a difference. We have work to do. There is room at the table for everyone. I love you to the moon and back!

Sincerely,
Dr. Katrina L. Sweet

About the Author

Dr. Katrina Lavette' Sweet is an energetic motivational speaker, teacher, and author with a genuine passion for women and youth. Her once tortured and defeated life drives her to spend the majority of her time advocating for youth and being a voice for those who are living a seemingly underprivileged and defeated life. She has been featured on the 700 club and various local and national radio stations. Additionally, Dr. Sweet enjoys sharing the Good News of the Gospel to those who are suffering, rejected, and afflicted. She provides comfort to the brokenhearted and announces liberty to the captives. As one who has been healed from rejection and abuse, she desires nothing more than to see women healed and walking in freedom and their divine purpose in life. She is an example of an individual who has taken her experiences to build other people up that have experienced similar struggles. One of her greatest strengths is teaching individuals how to exchange a victim's mentality for victory. Her first book, "Silent Screams From Within: A Woman Story of Tragedy to Triumph" was released in 2011. As she shares her healing from years of sexual, mental, and physical abuse, it gives people hope to believe again.

Dr. Sweet earned a BA in Criminal Justice from

North Carolina Wesleyan College, a MPA in Public Administration with a specialization in Government from Keller Graduate School of Management, and she has a PhD in Organization Management from Capella University. She is the CEO and Founder of PATCH, Inc. (Parents and Their Children), an advocacy organization that bring awareness of educational disparities and sexual abuse. She is also an Adjunct Professor at Colorado Technical University. Finally, Dr. Sweet currently resides in North Carolina. She is the proud parent of two, Tashika and Kevin. She is looking forward to God enlarging her territory as she continues to bring honor to Him and His Kingdom.

For additional information about Dr. Katrina Sweet or to invite her for a book signing or as a keynote speaker or presenter, please contact her at kls@ katrinasweet.com. You can also contact her at www. katrinasweet.com or www.klspatch.org.

REFERENCES

Baer, M, Abhijeet, K., Lenders, R., & Oldham, G. (2014). Intergroup competition as a double-edge sword: How sex composition regulates the effects of competition on group creativity. *Organization Science, Articles in Advance*, 1-7.

Björkqvist, K. (1994). Sex differences in physical, verbal, and indirect aggression: A review of recent research. *Sex Roles, 30,* 177-188.

Bjorkqvist, K., & Osterman, K. (2014). Does childhood physical punishment predispose to a victim personality". *Pediat Therapeut, 4* (190), 2161-0665.

Ellis, D. ((2014). *Why men don't come home after five.* Raleigh, NC: Pendium Publishing.

Heim, P., Murphy, S., & Golant, S. (2003). *In the company of women. Indirect aggression among women: Why we hurt each other and how to stop it.* New York, NY: Penguin Group

Rains, S. (2013). The nature of psychological reactance revisited: A meta-analytic review. *Human Communication Research, 39(1)*, 47-73.

Vaillancourt, T. (2013). Do human females use indirect aggression as an intrasexual competition strategy? *Philosophical Transaction of the Royal Society B: Biological Sciences, 368* (1631).

www.ingramcontent.com/pod-product-compliance
Lightning Source LLC
Chambersburg PA
CBHW031146250726
48655CB00002B/857